THIRTY-FIVE MONEY MAKING OR SAVING TIPS FOR HMO LANDLORDS

C. J. Haliburton

BA, DMS, Cert ED

HMO Landlord with over 20 years' experience, 130 HMOs and 800 tenants

www.hmodaddy.com

Copyright 2014 C. J. Haliburton

www.hmodaddy.com

The moral right of the author has been asserted.

All rights reserved. Apart from any fair dealing for the purposes of research or private study, or criticism or review, as permitted under the Copyright, Designs and Patents Act 1988, this publication may only be reproduced, stored or transmitted, in any form or by any means, with the prior permission in writing of the copyright owner, or in the case of the reprographic reproduction in accordance with the terms of licences issued by the Copyright Licensing Agency. Enquiries concerning reproduction outside those terms should be sent to the publisher.

HMO Daddy
14 Walsall Road
Wednesbury
West Midlands
WS10 9JL

Print Edition
ISBN: 978-1-326-12449-6
British Library Cataloguing in Publication Data.
A catalogue record for this book is available from the British Library.
Cover design, editing and proof-reading by Oxford Literary Consultancy.

CONTENTS

A NOTE OF CAUTION 5

TOP TIP 1: Fit Electric Card Meters to Each Rentable Room 7

TOP TIP 2: Add a Kitchenette to En Suite Rooms 11

TOP TIP 3: Fit Coin or Card Meters to Washing Machines 14

TOP TIP 4: Turn a Lounge into a Room 15

TOP TIP 5: Split a Large Bedroom into Two or More Bedrooms .. 18

TOP TIP 6: Turn a Room into a Self-Contained Room 20

TOP TIP 7: Charge an Administration Fee and Forget Deposits ... 23

TOP TIP 8: Fit Master Lock Systems 24

TOP TIP 9: Get Multiple Keys Cut at the Same Time and Number Them 26

TOP TIP 10: Buy a Key Cutter 27

TOP TIP 11: Fit a Fire Door 28

TOP TIP 12: Remove Central Heating or Don't Fit Central Heating 30

TOP TIP 13: Charge a Top-Up 33

TOP TIP 14: Fit LED Bulbs 36

TOP TIP 15: Fit LED Maintained Emergency Lights as Lights in Communal Areas 37

TOP TIP 16: Put a Standing Charge on Electric Meters 39

TOP TIP 17: Fit Carpet Tiles to Rooms 40

TOP TIP 18: Shop Around for Utilities 41

TOP TIP 19: Charge for Wi-Fi 43

TOP TIP 20: Use Trade Emulsion for Walls and Stain for Woodwork 44

TOP TIP 21: Review Building Insurance 46

TOP TIP 22: Manage Your HMO Yourself 49

TOP TIP 23: Go for Big HMOs 52

TOP TIP 24: Go for DSS 54

TOP TIP 25: Educate Your Tenants 56

TOP TIP 26: Shop Using the Web 58

TOP TIP 27: Charge Other Landlords a Tenant Finding Fee 59

TOP TIP 28: Charge Extra for Services and Furniture 60

TOP TIP 29: Charge tenants for storage 62

TOP TIP 30: Buy End of Range 63

TOP TIP 31: Charge a Tenancy Renewal Fee 64

TOP TIP 32: Don't Waste Money on Maintenance Contracts 65

TOP TIP 33: Increase the Rent for Problem Tenants 66

TOP TIP 34: Make Life Easy for Yourself 67

TOP TIP 35: Learn to Self-Evaluate 68

BONUS TIP 69

HMO DADDY RUNS COURSES 70

THE AUTHOR 71

I WANT TO HEAR FROM YOU 72

A NOTE OF CAUTION

Before implementing some of these fantastic money-making or saving tips, a note of caution—never, ever take anything away from your tenants or you will upset them and they will leave. Tenants rarely ever complain if you give or offer to sell them some additional facilities. Some of the tips, therefore, can only be done when your property is empty or when setting up your HMO. It is possible to introduce some of the tips into your HMO by giving existing tenants something for free and only charging new tenants, but do this with great sensitivity.

The following are mostly tips I have used. The extra income, costing and savings are applicable to my area in the West Midlands. You will have to adjust them to take into account your own situation.

I apologise that there is nothing about energy conservation apart from LED bulbs (see Top Tip 14) as I have not found that it saves money. I believe it is a massive con, but that is another story—see my book *HMO Daddy Reveals All.*

Enjoy!

C. J. Haliburton

TOP TIP 1
Fit Electric Card Meters to Each Rentable Room

Card meters cost about £60 to buy and around £100 to fit (see attached diagram). The average cost of electricity for my HMOs is £800 p.a. This will drop a massive 48% to £500 p.a. by the fitting of card meters. Even better, you can recover all your cost of supplying electricity from the sale of electric cards, and thus cover all your cost of supplying electricity. The cards are programmed only for your meters and cannot be purchased anywhere else.

There are two systems now available:

- The old system is where the card is made of cardboard and is single-use, and a new card is used each time.
- The new system uses digital meters. The digital meters card is plastic, like a credit card, and can be used multiple times.

The old and new meters cost about the same. However, the single-use cardboard cards cost about 20p and the multiple-use plastic cards cost about £1 each. If you assume the average HMO has six rooms, then the saving is a massive:

$$\textbf{Saving:} \quad \frac{£800 \text{ pa average electric bill}}{(£60 \text{ meters} + £100 \text{ to fit}) \times 6 \text{ rooms}} \times 100$$

$$= 83\% \text{ RETURN}$$

There is a net loss of £160 in the first year, then a massive saving of £800 or more if the cost of electricity increases in subsequent years.

NOTES:

I. A qualified electrician is required by law to do any electrical work, which would include fitting an electric card meter.
II. I often get asked about the communal areas. My experience is that very little electric is used in the communal areas.
III. My tenants rarely cook so it is not an issue. I have heard of landlords fitting coin-operated meters to cookers and showers, but I feel this is a bit OTT. The main source of electric use is electric heaters.
IV. You need to become aware that once you fit meters, some tenants will bypass the meters or run extension leads to the communal areas. Watch out for this.
V. Fitting meters can also improve your rent collection rate as the tenant has to regularly see you to buy electric cards.

HMO Daddy provides a competitive-priced starter pack using the digital meters—see www.hmodaddy.com for more information.

How to fit card meters to a room:

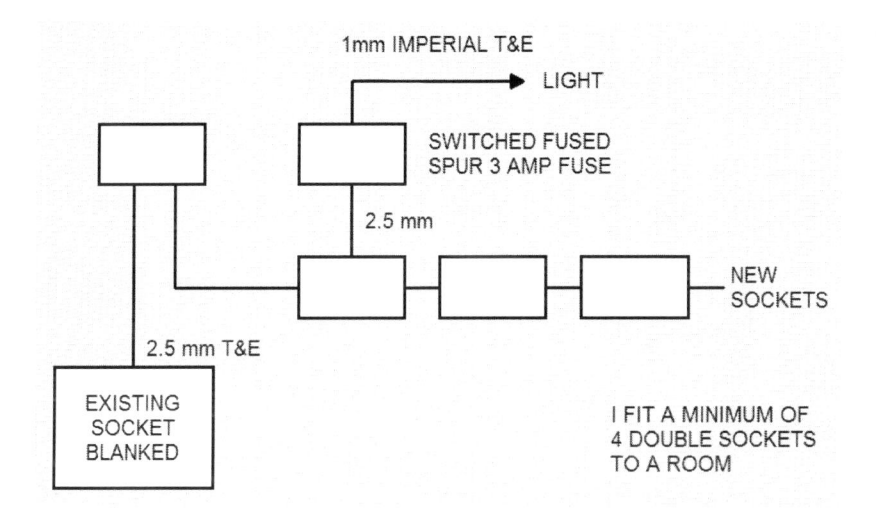

```
                    1mm IMPERIAL T&E
                    ┌──────────────▶ LIGHT
                    │
            ┌─────┐  SWITCHED FUSED
            │     │  SPUR 3 AMP FUSE
┌─────┐     │     │
│     │     │     │  2.5 mm
│     │     │     │
│     │     └──┬──┘
└──┬──┘        │                          NEW
   │     ┌──┐──┴─┌──┐──┌──┐──┌──┐ ─────── SOCKETS
   │     └──┘    └──┘  └──┘  └──┘
   │  2.5 mm T&E
┌──┴──────┐
│EXISTING │                    I FIT A MINIMUM OF
│SOCKET   │                    4 DOUBLE SOCKETS
│BLANKED  │                    TO A ROOM
└─────────┘
```

*Connect 2.5mm Imperial T&E to any one of your existing sockets and blank off all other sockets.

*Imperial T&E twin and earth electric cable, it is usually grey in colour.

- Fit card meter at a convenient spot in the room, no higher than five feet from the ground, so that the card can be used without having to stand on a chair or step. Some environmental health officers consider it unsafe if tenants need to use steps to access meters.
- If you wish, the light etc., can be run off the meter by spurring off a new socket and fitting a switched fused spur installed with a three amp fuse.
- The old and new digital card meters and the cards are obtainable from P & J Wales Meters (www.

pjwmeters.co.uk) for about £60 each + VAT plus P&P. The single-use cards cost about 20p each and the multi-use cards are about £1 each.

TOP TIP 2
Add a Kitchenette to En Suite Rooms

It costs me under £500 in parts and labour to fit a kitchenette to an en suite room. There is a big saving in the plumbing work as it is already there for the en suite. I don't use the pre-built kitchenettes as they are expensive. I have lost too many as they are made of metal, and most things made of metal walk in my properties!

I use a work surface that can be cut to any length to fit—the average is 1.2 metres—as well as a base unit, sink, taps, wall cupboards, shelf (all from Ikea); a microwave and kettle (from ASDA) and a fridge that is usually second-hand. This is along with fittings and electrics. You need to fit an extractor fan for ventilation. The total cost is about £500.

The benefit of adding a kitchenette to an en suite room is that you can now get the one-bedroom rate for Housing Benefit, providing the tenants are over 35 years old. There are some exceptions to this rule where under-35s can get the one-bedroom rate (see below). The room, as soon as it has its own cooking facilities and bathroom, will for most areas give you a 50% increase in rent for Housing Benefit and a good 10% uplift for working tenants. Strictly speaking for Housing Benefit purposes, the tenant does not need an en suite bathroom or kitchenette, only exclusive use of a bathroom and cooking facilities.

I find this gives a massive increase in rent of:

Saving: $\dfrac{52 \text{ weeks} \times £30}{£500} \times 100 = $ **312% RETURN**
Cost:

This gives a net income of £1,060 in the first year, and a massive £1,560 extra income or more as rent increase in subsequent years.

NOTES:

I. You should check with your local Building Control Department whether you need building control approval to fit a kitchenette. My view is that you do not need any as there is no new plumbing.
II. A qualified electrician should fit the electrics.
III. Whether it is a planning issue is contentious. It is best to say it is a tea-making facility, and have a communal kitchen, to avoid any suggestion that you have turned the room into a flat for which you would need planning approval. See my book *Planning and HMOs* for more on this, available at www.hmodaddy.com.
IV. The Housing Standards Department will often require improved fire precautions if you introduce cooking facilities into a room. This is not particularly onerous—usually the council will require the smoke detector in the room to be changed to a heat detector, because if the tenants use the microwave it could result in the smoke detector being activated, thereby causing false alarms. I

have never known a microwave to activate a smoke detector unless a tenant puts metal in the microwave, which they regularly do and this causes it to burn out! To provide early warning of smoke, you are also often required to fit a self-contained smoke detector in the room fitted with a hush button to temporarily stop it sounding. (This sounds only within the room, but they are so loud that the rest of the house will hear it.) Some councils also insist that you fit a fire blanket wherever there are cooking facilities. For the cost, I don't bother arguing, but I don't see the point and believe they present a danger to users.

V. A microwave and kettle count as cooking facilities for the purpose of getting the one-bedroom rate from Housing Benefit. Please refer to my case* against Wolverhampton City Council on this point when the tribunal held that a sink, fridge, microwave and kettle were considered sufficient for cooking facilities.

Some of the exemptions to the over-35s rule for claiming Housing Benefit at the single-bed rate are:

- Couples of any age
- Care leavers, up to 22 years old
- Violent offenders
- Stayed in a hostel(s) at any time for a total of three months
- Claiming higher level Disability Living Allowance (DLA)

*Available from my website, www.hmodaddy.com.

TOP TIP 3
Fit Coin or Card Meters to Washing Machines

As soon as you charge for something an odd thing happens—its use drastically reduces. So do not expect anything like the previous use to continue. By charging, not only will you bring in an income but you will save on wear and tear on the machine, electric and water usage. Before I fitted a meter to a washing machine in one property, the machine was used 24/7. Now, it rarely gets used.

The meters you fit are not the same as for metering rooms. You need to fit timer meters that are usually more expensive than card meters. The meters cost about £90 each and fitting costs about £60. A qualified electrician must fit the meter as it is electrical work. I charge £2 per wash, but most landlords charge about £3. Assuming you have six tenants in your HMO, and they wash their clothes once a week, then this gives a massive income of:

$$\frac{\textbf{Income:} \quad \text{£3 x 6 tenants x 52 weeks}}{\textbf{Cost:} \quad \text{£150 (£90 meter + £60 fitting)}} \times 100$$

$$= \textbf{624\% RETURN}$$

This gives a phenomenal net increase in income of £786 in the first year, then a massive £936 or more in subsequent years.

You can also fit a meter to a dryer with probably a smaller return. I fit separate dryers rather than washer-dryers, as I find I get fewer problems with two separate machines.

TOP TIP 4
Turn a Lounge into a Room

Depending on what your tenants want, you may be wasting a significant source of income in providing a lounge. I find my tenants do not use lounges for their intended purpose and do not take responsibility for it. I, therefore, do not now supply one. However, I would be very careful with an existing HMO and would check with my tenants before unilaterally turning it into another lettable room as the last thing you want is to upset your tenants. This is something you do when the property is empty or almost empty.

RETURN:

In my area, a room will attract about £65 pw. Apart from fitting a lock, and furnishings if you furnish your rooms, it will cost very little, say £200. This will give the following return:

Income: $\dfrac{£65 \times 52 \text{ weeks}}{£200} \times 100 =$ **1,690% RETURN**
Cost:

This gives a phenomenal net increase in income of £3,180 in the first year. In subsequent years, it gives a massive return of £3,380 or more as rent increase.

NOTES:

I. Councils have space standards for rooms. Under the standards set by some councils, a bedroom must be 100 sq ft/10 sq m if no lounge or dining kitchen is provided. A room can be 65 sq ft /6.5 sq m if a lounge is provided. Any requirement to provide a bedroom larger than 65 sq ft is only guidance and not law, and enforcement is variable. Understand that councils can ask landlords to do whatever they want—e.g. providing every tenant with a bathroom. But if they try to enforce it the landlord can appeal, and it is for the appeal tribunal to decide if what is asked for is reasonable, except where it is the law. The law says you need a bathroom for every five tenants.

II. By increasing the number of rooms, you may raise the concerns of the planners. Appreciate that the Planning Use Class 4 up to six sharing is not set in stone—see my book, *HMOs & Planning* available from www.hmodaddy.com.

III. If building works are required, you may need Building Control approval. The room should comply with your council's space standards, have natural light and an opening window.

IV. If the property is licensed, then you will need to apply for a licence variation.

V. If your council insists that you have a lounge, it can be anywhere—for example, a building in the back garden! One of my councils agrees with me that lounges are not needed by tenants and cause problems, and they are happy for me not to supply them, but this is by no means universal. Remember you can always appeal to the First Tier Appeal Tribunal—Property Division (previously the Residential Property Tribunal) if your council pushes you over this matter.

VI. I have seen no cases regarding lounges. All the cases so far insist on a minimum bedroom size of 65 sq ft/ 6.5 sq m.

TOP TIP 5
Split a Large Bedroom into Two or More Bedrooms

Depending on what you find is wanted by your tenants, and whether they are prepared to pay for it, this top tip may be a good way to increase your income considerably. My experience is that most tenants do not like small rooms so you may be reducing market demand if you adopt this strategy. However, what is small? The law says a room must be a minimum of 65 sq ft /6.5 sq m and this is small. Although we imprison people in cells of 32 sq ft /3.2 sq m for up to 23 hours a day and this is considered humane. People are sent to prison as a punishment, not *for* punishment. My experience is that I find tenants tend to remain longer in units of over 100 sq ft /10 sq m, but it is rarely viable for me to provide this level of accommodation. Again, it is a question of try it and see.

I have demand for small rooms from Department of Social Security (DSS) tenants under the age of 35, and workers who have just moved into the area who require cheap accommodation. With DSS tenants, there is a limit on how much rent is paid by Housing Benefit, and the tenants have themselves very little to pay anything above what Housing Benefit will pay. In effect, you have a market where the rent is fixed for a certain sector, and there is a very restricted opportunity to charge more.

RETURN:

I charge £65 pw for a room, and the cost of splitting the room will depend on what is involved. I can rarely do it for less than £1,000. This will give a massive:

$$\frac{\text{Income: } £65 \times 52 \text{ weeks}}{\text{Cost: } £1,000} \times 100 = \textbf{338\% RETURN}$$

This gives a fantastic net increase in income of £2,380 in the first year, and an enormous £3,380 or more as rents increase in subsequent years.

NOTES:

I. Strictly speaking, splitting a room is a Building Control matter. Historically, the Building Control Department has shown little interest in small works, but this is changing. They are now showing a lot more interest in this type of small works. Check with your council first as the splitting of a room may trigger sound-proofing works, etc. Each room needs natural light and an opening window.
II. A qualified electrician should do the electrical work.
III. Whether splitting a room is a planning issue is contentious. It will probably not cause any problems, providing that the number of lettable rooms is about six. See my book *HMOs and Planning* for more on this – available at www.hmodaddy.com.

TOP TIP 6
Turn a Room into a Self-Contained Room

My experience is that self-contained rooms, especially if done well, are much easier to let. As I referred to in Top Tip 2, a self-contained room will attract a 50% increase in rent in my area if let to a Housing Benefit tenant. Whether the same applies in your area depends on demand and rent levels. Often, you have to try it and see. I had a friend who on nothing more than a whim changed her tired 'room' HMO (in an area of oversupply of rooms) into high-quality self-contained units. She was amazed at the demand and rent she could achieve—almost double the room rent. She initially thought she would only get 10% or 20% more, but tenants were saying, "I want it—how much?" The rent was progressively increased as each new room became available, until the final letting was almost double what she charged as a room—i.e. the same size unit, but now with its own en suite and kitchenette. The rent increases are best done when the existing tenants leave, then the new tenants are charged a higher rent.

To turn a whole house into self-contained units may be a step too far, but you could try with one room to start with. My model of self-contained units is to provide a small en suite 2ft 6in by 6 ft 6 in /0.7 m x 2m, about the size of a large wardrobe. The kitchenette is small—about 4 ft in length/1.2m, with a small sink, microwave, kettle, fridge, base and wall cupboard. You can buy ready-made units; they are much more expensive, but look good.

RETURN:

Converting a room into a self-contained unit is not cheap —it costs me on average £5,000. In my area, a room will fetch from £65 pw depending on size while I charge £100 pw for a self-contained room. Assuming I was getting £75 pw for a large room, then that room turned into a studio will produce an extra £25pw. But more importantly, you can attract a better class of tenants who will reduce bad debts, voids, damage and administration. You will get a massive:

$$\frac{\textbf{Income: } £25 \times 52 \text{ weeks}}{\textbf{Cost: } £5,000} \times 100 = \textbf{26\% RETURN}$$

This means a net loss of £3,700 in the first year, but once paid for (which will take 3.8 years) this will give an increased income of £1,300 or more as rents increase in subsequent years.

NOTES:

I. You should check with your local Building Control Department whether you need approval to fit a kitchenette and en suite. My take is that you do not need permission if there is no new drainage needed.
II. A qualified electrician should fit the electrics.

III. Fitting en suites is not normally a planning issue, although whether fitting a kitchenette is a planning issue is contentious. Best to say it is a tea-making facility and have a communal kitchen to avoid any suggestion that you have turned the room into a flat which would need planning approval. See my book *Planning and HMOs* for more on this at www.hmodaddy.com.

IV. Many Council Housing Standards Departments will require improved fire precautions if you introduce cooking facilities into a room. This is not particularly onerous. Usually, the council will require the smoke detector in the room to be changed to a heat detector, because if the tenants use the microwave it could result in the smoke detector being activated thereby causing false alarms. I have never known a microwave to activate a smoke detector unless a tenant puts metal in the microwave, which they regularly do and this causes it to burn out.

V. To provide early warning of smoke, also fit a self-contained smoke detector in the room fitted with a hush button to temporarily stop it sounding. It sounds only within the room, but they are so loud that the rest of the house will hear it. Some councils also insist that you fit a fire blanket whenever there are cooking facilities. For the cost, I don't bother arguing, but I don't see the point and believe their use in a fire puts a tenant at an unacceptable risk.

TOP TIP 7
Charge an Administration Fee and Forget Deposits

Most letting agents charge an administration fee, yet very few landlords do. Before the Tenancy Deposit Scheme came in, I had read and rejected taking deposits as a potential liability. Subsequent events have sadly proved me right. Luckily, few tenants have taken the opportunity to sue their landlords for the deposit plus three times the original deposit, which many could if they only realised the opportunity. Also see my article 'How to Avoid the Tenancy Deposit Scheme and Turn it into a Marketing and Financial Advantage' now re-published in my new book *HMO Daddy Reveals All* available from www.hmodaddy.com. So instead of bothering with a deposit, charge an administration fee that you can keep. Make sure you clearly state it is an administration fee and it is not refundable. I charge £175 administration fee for a studio and I know of those who charge far more.

RETURN:

Say you charge £200 and your tenants stay on average for six months, and there are six tenants in your HMO, then you have made an extra 6 x 2 x £200 = £2,400 per year per HMO. This is more profit than some landlords make on their HMOs.

TOP TIP 8
Fit Master Lock Systems

A master lock system is where one master key opens every door in your properties. The tenants have a key that will only open their door. When you only have one HMO it does not matter so much; you can cope with a dozen keys. When you have three or more HMOs, then it becomes a nightmare. Most systems will allow you to buy additional locks as you need them, and can start with as little as £15 per lock if you use rim locks (sometimes referred to as night latches).

I do not recommend the use of rim locks, as the tenant can easily lock themselves out as the door automatically locks if closed. You can get deadbolt night latches, but I find they are more expensive and ugly compared to the system I use. With an HMO, the doors must always have thumb-turn locks on the inside, so the tenant can get out of the room or house without a key. The cost of a master lock system is completely outweighed by the convenience.

I use the euro lock system, the same system of lock that is used on UPVC doors. When I refer to a lock, I am only meaning the bit that the key is put in, called the 'lock barrel'. The locking mechanism is not the same as a UPVC door, but is a simple deadlock. See my website www.hmodaddy.com for more information.

RETURN:

Unquantifiable, and the convenience immeasurable.

Of all the tips I have given, this is the one that other HMO landlords appear to appreciate the most!

TOP TIP 9
Get Multiple Keys Cut at the Same Time and Number Them

By getting multiple keys cut at the same time, this not only saves you time in the long run, but usually you can negotiate a bulk purchase from the key cutters—so saving money. Tenants are forever losing their keys or forget to take their keys with them, so you will need spare keys. I always change the lock to rooms whenever a tenant leaves, and recirculate the lock later, so any spare keys I may have for the lock are not wasted. The cutting of multiple keys will save time and money, and makes life easier.

While having the keys cut, number the key barrel and the keys with the same number. This will make finding and matching keys so much easier. When getting the keys cut, take the lock barrel with you so you can test that the keys work while you are at the key cutters. Those of you who have had keys cut badly, and experienced the frustration and time wasted in going back to have them checked, will appreciate this tip. Have three times the number of keys cut to the number of occupiers in the property, though less if there are above 12 occupiers, as I find the front door lock gets changed before the keys are used for security reasons.

RETURN:

Unquantifiable in time saved, stress avoided and simplicity.

TOP TIP 10
Buy a Key Cutter

Once you have over 40 tenants, you should consider buying a key cutting machine. This is providing you have not fitted high-security locks which cannot be easily cut and require expensive equipment to cut. For under £1,000 you can buy a new cutter, or if you can find one, you can buy a second-hand key cutter for substantially less. They are very easy to use and it takes only minutes to cut a key—this will save £2 to £5 per key you cut. Have a quick calculation as to how many keys you need to cut and see if it will be worthwhile investing in a key cutter.

RETURN:

I estimate I save over £1K a year cutting my own keys. This is more if I price in labour in the time spent going to get keys cut.

TOP TIP 11
Fit a Fire Door

One of an HMO landlord's typical comments is, "Fit a door, fit a fire door" as they have realised that they are cheap and much more serviceable than an ordinary door. A fire door is much stronger than an ordinary door and is a lot more soundproof. It is much harder to break a fire door and they only cost from £17 to buy. As most fire doors are a little bit thicker than an ordinary door, the door stops in the door frame need to be rebated or if screwed, repositioned. If a new door frame is required or it is a new door entry, then you can buy a fire door frame. The fire door frame has the grooves already cut ready to fit intumescent strips, which some councils require to be fitted.

A fire door should only be painted with fire retardant paint if it is to keep its fire rating. Many landlords will just stain them to get around this problem, using the same economically-priced stain used for fences. To make it even easier, you can pre-stain the doors before fitting using a roller, which makes the job of painting the door quicker and easier.

RESULT: For what you could be paying for an ordinary door you get a longer lasting and better product.

With upmarket HMOs, consider spending more and getting

the white paneled fire doors. They cost about £40 but look so much better than the cheaper doors.

RETURN:

Unquantifiable.

TOP TIP 12
Remove Central Heating or Don't Fit Central Heating

I find it bizarre that with the few HMO properties I offer without central heating it makes no difference in the ability to let, retention rate or rent I can charge. It has the added benefit that the tenants do not complain about the heating not working or their rooms not being hot enough. The main cause of complaints I receive in the winter months is about the central heating. The more significant benefit of not providing central heating is that it saves me about £1,200 per year per property. Where I provide central heating I find tenants complain if it is not on 24/7, so the heating ends up being on all the time. The cost of heating is included in the rent; I long ago gave up trying to charge separately for heating or having a fair use policy.

Where central heating is not supplied, an HMO landlord is required to provide a fixed form of heating. Most landlords fit panel heaters that screw to the wall. You can buy panel heaters from about £20 each, and it costs me about £30 in labour and materials to fit one. There are some very expensive types of panel heaters about, costing in excess of £200 each, but I fail to understand why they are cheaper to operate. A kilowatt of electric becomes a kilowatt of heat whichever way you do it, a bit like a pint of water is still only a pint of water however much the pint glass costs.

Where I find not providing central heating does not work is where central heating is already installed. I tried it a few times last year with new properties and the result was a disaster. There were two problems. The first was where we used the heating to dry out the house—the property had been empty for years so the heating was on when the tenants viewed, though we had clearly told them that the heating was not included. This did not stop the tenants demanding that I supplied it.

The second was that tenants would turn the heating on. The heating was securely locked away, but tenants would break in and switch the boiler on.

The answer, it appears, is to take the heating out. Understand that if you have a central heating system installed, then by law it must work, but the landlord does not have to pay for it. If Housing Standards ask you, you only have to say that it is for the tenants to pay and they have not paid. The other issue is that you have to provide controllable 24/7 heating. I have had a Housing Officer demand, where I was paying for the heating, for it to be on to heat the house for one person who happened to be in the property at the time of the inspection and she was not even a tenant! That she was a scantily dressed, young, pretty female had nothing to do with it! I would have told her to put her coat on, but the housing standard officer in his wisdom took a different view.

There is currently no requirement upon a landlord to provide an economical form of heating; I think it will be coming, but not soon. If you are going to fit electric heaters then you should meter each room (see Top Tip 1), otherwise your electric bill will go through the roof. With meters, there is strangely not much of an increase in the electric used where the central heating is not provided by the landlord. This is probably because the tenants have to pay for it themselves and they choose to wear a sweater instead.

I find not providing central heating saves a massive:

$$\frac{\textbf{Income:} \quad £1{,}200 \text{ cost of heating per year}}{\textbf{Cost:} \quad 6 \text{ heaters @ } (£20 \text{ each} + £30 \text{ each to fit})} \times 100$$

$$= \ \textbf{800\% RETURN}$$

This gives a net saving of £900 in the first year, and then £1,200 or more if the cost of heating increases in subsequent years.

The downside is that your property may have damp and mould, be cold and possibly unattractive in winter to potential tenants. Tenants tend to blame the landlord for mould, and it could give rise to issues.

TOP TIP 13
Charge a Top-Up

This tip only applies to landlords with Housing Benefit tenants. You may not realise it, but a landlord does not have to charge the Housing Benefit rate—they can charge more or even less. Whether to charge more is down to the landlord's assessment. I oddly, rarely find that the charging of top-ups is an issue. Getting it is another matter, but even if only 50% of your tenants pay, you will be better off. I find that with relentless effort, over 90% of my tenants pay and this represents for me a good 10% increase in rent received. To get paid a top-up with bad payers, you need to collect it on the day that the tenant gets their Giro payment, which is every fortnight. Go and collect the top-up on the day they are paid—do not leave it until the day after, as it will have been spent.

How much to charge is again up to you. I charge between £5 pw to £15 pw collected fortnightly. Anything more than £15 pw from an unemployed tenant will not work; they will often promise but rarely pay. Over half of my tenants pay their top-up without being asked to pay. They come and pay it at my rent office.

Charging a top-up has the advantage of not only the increased income but also:

- Closer contact with your tenants—if they are paying out of their own pocket instead of it all being paid by Housing Benefit, they will want a good service, and highlight problems with the property which may prevent problems becoming worse.
- You will know if your tenants have left. One of the problems I find with Housing Benefit tenants is that they are reluctant to tell you they are leaving; you just discover they have left. Once they discover the tenant has left, Housing Benefit departments will usually recover all the benefits paid after the tenant left. They are highly motivated to reclaim benefits because they get extra payment for doing so. I have numerous reclaims and a few for over 12 months' rent, which is a substantial sum of money!

The defences you have to a reclaim are:

- If the rent was paid directly to the tenant, or,
- You could not have reasonably have known that the tenant was no longer entitled to Housing Benefit.

Housing Benefit departments reclaim an overpayment by automatically deducting it from the rent paid for the tenant or they invoice you, the landlord. A very good defence to reclaim is if the tenant is paying you a top-up. I use an NCR book and so I can provide a copy of the receipts. If the tenant is paying a fortnightly top-up, then this is good evidence that they are in occupation. The Housing Benefit department has never ever pursued a repayment claim where I have shown receipts for top-ups during the period where they say the tenant was not in occupation.

RETURN:

Up to 10% or more increase in rent and a more effective business.

TOP TIP 14
Fit LED Bulbs

LED bulbs have two advantages:

1. LED bulbs cost about one-tenth of the cost of the old filament light bulbs to run and about half the cost of low energy bulbs.
2. LED bulbs last far longer than both the old filament bulb and low energy bulbs. I have been using LED lighting for over a year now, and I have never had to change a LED light. I appreciate that low energy bulbs have been around for a few years, and so it is not a fair comparison. I will review this in a few years.

LED bulbs and fittings are now coming down considerably in price if you shop around for them. I use CPC, an online supplier, for my bulbs (www.cpc.farnell.com). To quantify the saving is almost impossible as the use of lighting is so variable. I have seen some of the calculations used by suppliers and they are questionably on the high side.

RETURN:

Unquantifiable, but definitely a saving.

TOP TIP 15
Fit LED Maintained Emergency Lights as Lights in Communal Areas

I fit 24/7 lighting to my hallways, stairs, landings and communal areas. I think it looks warmer, as well as giving security and a good feel to the property, so this tip may not appeal to those who adopt a different approach and like to switch off. Long ago, I stopped using bayonet lights in communal areas as the bulbs kept getting stolen. I used 2D bulbs, which were the early form of energy-efficient lighting. Housing Standards then came along and insisted that I fitted emergency lighting in case there was a fire and the power failed so the tenants could not find their way out. This requirement makes little sense to me because:

1. What was the chance of a fire and a power failure at the same time?
2. Tenants lived there and knew the way out.

With so many things you just do it, so why not embrace it and save money by doing so? LED emergency lights can be purchased for as little as £12 + VAT from CPC an online distributor (www.cpc.farnell.com). Emergency lights can be either 'non-maintained' which means they only come on if there is a power failure or 'maintained' which means they remain on all the time. The emergency lights only use 5 watts of power, that is 1/20th of a 100 watt bulb. So for less money than it would cost for most light fittings, you can have

24/7 lighting using maintained emergency lighting for about £5 p.a. per light fitting and you only need to fit one light, instead of a light plus an emergency light. Another way of looking at it is to compare what it would cost to operate a 40 watt bulb for three hours a day with 24/7 LED lighting. The 40 watt bulbs will need changing regularly and will go missing.

Even if you fit low energy bulbs, then the equivalent would only give 15 hours of lighting per day for the same cost. Normally, you will fit a light and an emergency light in the same area.

RETURN:

- Fit only one light fitting instead of two.
- Cheaper light fittings.
- Enhanced safety and comfort.
- Possible cost saving.

TOP TIP 16
Put a Standing Charge on Electric Meters

See my Top Tip about fitting electric meters. These meters can also be programmed to charge a weekly standing charge. By charging, say £1 or £2 per week, you can directly improve your bottom line. This will also, providing you keep good records of electric card sales, give an indication of whether a tenant is in occupation or fiddling the meter (unfortunately something which is not uncommon).

Say you have 120 tenants each paying £2 pw, this will give £12,500 pa clear profit for no extra work.

RETURN:

A worthwhile increase on your bottom line.

TOP TIP 17
Fit Carpet Tiles to Rooms

Using tiles is not cheaper than carpet. It does, however, make the task a simple DIY job to do. When refurbishing the room you only have to replace stained areas, so on balance it is cheaper to do. I will not spend time here explaining how to carpet tile a floor—there are plenty of DIY manuals that explain this. It is the principle I am establishing. Shop around for a good reasonable supply of tiles and off you go. It will take less than an hour to tile a room. Once you have offset the cost against the cost of a carpet layer, arranging access, etc. you are quids in.

If you are so minded get used tiles. The web is fantastic for this—you can find suppliers of ex-commercial tiles at a fraction of their original cost. They are almost indestructible and seem to last forever. I accept they are not to everyone's taste and may not be appropriate for upmarket HMOs.

RETURN:

Difficult to quantify.

TOP TIP 18
Shop Around for Utilities

There is a strange myth doing the property circuit that just because a company says it is the cheapest supplier for gas and electric that it is the cheapest! I would like to kill this myth—IT IS NOT THE CHEAPEST. I have done the unthinkable by comparing prices, and I find I can usually get a good 20% saving by shopping around. It gets even worse: the difference I have discovered between the cheapest and most expensive supplier is almost three times the cost! When you consider that the average gas and electric bill for an HMO is £2,000 pa, then this means I could be paying as much as £6,000 p.a. If I did not shop around, it would cost a good £4,000 more a year—the price of an all-inclusive luxury holiday for two!

When I ask participants on my courses if anyone knows the cost of gas and electricity, rarely does anyone have a clue. It is as if it is a state secret. If you do not know, you cannot compare. It does not help that some utility companies have standing charges, cashback, etc. I find it bizarre how some people's minds work. I once tried to get a lady to change suppliers—it would have saved her over £200 p.a.—but she refused as the utility company gave her a cashback every year of about £100! You can give me £200 and I will give you £100 back any day—please create an orderly queue!

One of the benefits of joining HMO Daddy's group is that I

have negotiated for members a special price with suppliers; I employ a consultant to do the job of negotiating to get the cheapest supplier. As I am a volume user, I pay the utilities on over 100 HMOs. I can usually get a better price and I also get this price for my members—see my website wwww.hmodaddy.com for details. Alternatively, spend a few days shopping around and I think you will find that you will save a whopping 20% which will represent over £400 pa on an average gas and electricity bill for an HMO.

RETURN:

A saving of at least £400 per year per property.

TOP TIP 19
Charge for Wi-Fi

When installing Wi-Fi for the first time, you can make an extra charge. We charge each tenant £7 pcm for Wi-Fi and give the tenant the code to access the Internet, which regularly changes to stop it being misused. Most of the top hotels do the same and charge for Wi-Fi, and often charge an awful lot more. You will find that it will cause ill will and might result in you losing tenants if you introduce charges to existing tenants who have previously had Wi-Fi for free. Do it for new tenants only, or start from when the house is empty.

The advantage of charging for Wi-Fi is that not only will it hopefully cover the cost of the Internet and phone line, but it gives you another source of income. To take a bit of the pressure off you when the Wi-Fi goes down, you can say to the tenants that they do not have to pay for it. This is better than them refusing to pay the rent! I find that a breakdown in Wi-Fi connection is the most aggressively complained about issue, even dwarfing the failure of central heating and hot water.

RETURN:

Difficult to quantify.

TOP TIP 20
Use Trade Emulsion for Walls and Stain for Woodwork

It is often difficult to get a reasonably priced and quality tradesperson to do redecorating. A freshly-painted room looks so much better and is easier to let. It is often simpler to do the job yourself as it is easy and quick to do. To do this, keep the paint to trade paints which are also so much more economical. Trade paint costs a fraction of the cost of the paints provided for the consumer market.

Another tip, if you like the Apple Blossom or Pink Haze etc. look, is to add a tiny amount of green or pink emulsion to a tub of trade paint and you will get the same effect for a fraction of the cost. Once you have got the shade you want, make a note of the amount of paint added so you can repeat it again.

I use white on ceilings and magnolia for the walls. Though to ensure simplicity and speed, I recommend using only one colour, i.e. white for the walls and ceiling. The starkness of the white can be ameliorated by adding a couple of pictures.

To make painting the woodwork quick and easy, use the stain you put on fences. Don't use creosote—there's nothing wrong with the stuff, it just stinks; a smell you do not want for your rooms. Wood stain is water-based, so is easy to use and dries much quicker than gloss paint. The overall effect of brown woodwork is rather classical and it gives a slightly bohemian look. It does not matter as long as it is presentable, quick and cheap to do. I can redecorate a room in a couple of hours—redecorate in the morning and it is ready to let in the afternoon, once you have systemized the process. It is also good exercise as well: you are bending and stretching and so it saves on gym fees and I find that it gives me enormous satisfaction!

RETURN:

Difficult to quantify.

TOP TIP 21
Review Building Insurance

When I do a rent-to-rent, I always offer as part of the deal to pay for the building insurance—why? Because I find I pay on average one-third of what the owner is paying and it stops any discussion as to who pays. I find it incredible what other landlords—who are often very tight over what they spend on property and/or who consider themselves to be good business people and negotiators—pay for insurance. If you asked them: "Would you pay more for a property when you could get a similar property, perhaps missing the 'bells and whistles' for a third of the price?" they would laugh at you. But they do it all the time with insurance.

I accept that insurance is often an emotional purchase, your comfort blanket—see the section on insurance in my book *How to Become a Multi-Millionaire HMO Landlord* available via www.hmodaddy.com.

One of the benefits of joining HMO Daddy's group is that I have negotiated for my members a special price with a broker. As I have a large portfolio, I have negotiated a very good deal—see my website www.hmodaddy.com for details of my membership group. Alternatively, spend a few days shopping around and you will find that you can make a considerable saving. One of the benefits of joining a landlord association (see list below) is that they provide competitive insurance for landlords, although not as good as I can.

RETURN:

2/3 of your current premium per property. I estimate I save over £160 per year per property.

LANDLORD ASSOCIATION GROUPS:

RLA – Residential Landlords Association

Telephone: 0161 962 0010
Fax : 0845 665 1845

Website: www.rla.co.uk

Email: info@rla.org.uk

1 Roebuck Lane
Sale
Manchester
M33 7SY

NLA – National Landlords Association

Telephone: 020 7840 8900

Website: www.landlords.org.uk

Email: info@landlords.org.uk

National Landlords Association
22-26 Albert Embankment
London
SE1 7TJ

SLA – Southern Landlords Association

Telephone: 0845 475 35 83

Website: southernlandlords.org

Email: info@southernlandlords.org

GRL – Guild of Residential Landlords

Tel: 01423 873399 or 08453700107

Website: www.landlordsguild.com

Email: enquiry@landlordsguild.com

51 Leadhall Lane
Harrogate
HG2 9NJ

TOP TIP 22
Manage Your HMO Yourself

Yes, you can if you are very lucky get others to successfully manage your HMOs, but:

1. If you haven't done it yourself, how would you recognise or appreciate whether they are doing the job well or not?
2. It does not take that much time to manage the properties yourself if you set it up correctly in the first place, which usually means:
   - Keep it local—if you keep it local, you can easily and quickly check the property. If your tenants see you around regularly, they are less likely to play up and you can sense what is going on.
   - Let to professionals—or I would prefer to classify these as tenants with excellent credit records, identifiable by having good credit cards. These people have a credit status they need and want to protect, and so have a very low default rate. The problem is that you are fishing in the same pool as the majority of all other landlords, and unless you are very competitively priced or in an area of high demand, expect high voids until you get your target tenants. The typical scenario with those who adopt this strategy is that faced with a long void, they weaken and let to a 'very nice' person of uncertain credit status and they turn out to be the tenant from hell. The meaning of the phrase "a void is the

cheapest option" becomes clear as the good tenants leave and the HMO is trashed.
- Most hands-on landlords have developed an intuition for selecting the 'right' tenant, who is not in the normal sense creditworthy—maybe from overseas and so not able to be credit-checked. Most landlords or letting agents will not entertain such tenants, and this is where the small landlord creates a profitable 'niche' market.

3. When letting to the DSS section of the market (unemployed tenants, also known as Housing Benefit tenants) you will usually have to manage the property yourself, as few letting agents will deal with this type of tenant. To do this, you need to thoroughly understand the Housing Benefit system, and be very tenacious with the Housing Benefit department and with your tenants. Expect to have to educate your Housing Benefit departments and mount appeals to get what you are legally entitled to. You have to get it 100% right, whereas your Housing Benefit department, on the other hand, can be as inefficient as they want. My *Operating Standards* available at www.hmodaddy.com gives some very good basic advice on how to handle Housing Benefit tenants and the system.

4. Knowing how to do it yourself means you are beholden to no one. You could sack your agent or staff and manage your own properties should your agents or staff not be up to standard.

5. It is far more profitable to do it yourself—you will save

far more than the 10%, 12%, 15% etc. plus VAT that the letting agency charge, as they will bill you as extras for things you can do yourself for far less, and you will probably do it very much better as you will have the self-interest.
6. I estimate that by doing it yourself you will add well in excess of 20% of your potential rental income to your profit.

RETURN:

An extra 20% plus of your potential rental income on your bottom line!

TOP TIP 23
Go for Big HMOs

The return for a 10-bed HMO is three or four times the return from a five-bed HMO—not quite exponential returns, but well worth the extra effort. See the following examples:

Studios ->>	6	12	18
Acquisition*	£100K	£130K	£155K
Renovation	£60K	£120K	£180K
TOTAL COST	£160K	£250K	£335K
Utilities	£3,600 pa	£4,500 pa	£5,500 pa
Mortgage	£9,600 pa	£13,200 pa	£17,100 pa
Gross Rent	£31,200 pa	£62,400 pa	£93,600 pa
Net Rent	£18,000 pa	£44,700 pa	£71,000 pa

*This is for my area in the West Midlands.

The benefits of big HMOs:

- Massive cash-flow that will make an enormous difference to your bottom line.
- There is often little competition for large properties in need of work.

- Easy to manage—all rooms in one place.
- Potential for massive cash back on remortgaging.

RETURN:

Quadruple plus your rental profit for double your investment.

N.B: Appreciate that rental profit is only part of what you can make. Often, capital appreciation dwarfs this in the long term, and this is where owning a lot of houses can be a benefit. A large HMO is unlikely to rise in value as fast as a house will, but you can never predict with this!

TOP TIP 24
Go for DSS

DSS, also known as unemployed or benefit tenants, is a market many landlords shun without assessing it properly. Like all markets, there are different sectors which vary. I agree that the majority of the DSS market has challenging, demanding and often vulnerable tenants, but there is one section which many other landlords and I have identified as their very best tenants to have. These tenants are the over-50s who have worked most of their lives, but are now unemployed, usually because they have not been able to adapt to a changing market or they lack the skills now in demand. Often they have owned their own property and are recently divorced, their wife having kept the property and evicted them. The children have grown up.

The majority of this group make my ideal tenants as:

1. They stay for life—no turnover, re-letting costs or voids.
2. They are undemanding, grateful you have housed them, take responsibility for looking after the property, and rarely want anything or the property renovating.
3. Rent can, depending on the area, be more or comparable to what you can get for working tenants.

My question is: why would you not go for tenants who stay for life and are undemanding when you get the same or more rent? I find it a shame that many landlords go for what they love to call "professional tenants" for snobby reasons.

RETURN:

Hassle-free letting!

TOP TIP 25
Educate Your Tenants

Charge for unnecessary call-outs by your tenants. Establish your ground rules right from the start in writing—no messing about, be polite, friendly but firm. List what the tenant is expected to do, and make it very clear that if they fail to do it and then call expecting you to sort it out, you will charge them. Explain that if the tenant calls you out, for example for the following reasons:

- Lost keys
- The electric has tripped out
- The gas or electric prepay has not been topped up

then you will charge them a pre-agreed set fee. I charge £25 per call-out, which I threaten to charge but rarely do, as I feel it is too much to charge a DSS or unemployed tenant, as are the majority of my tenants. However, I discovered an HMO landlord who lets to working tenants in London and charges £140 per call-out, and ruthlessly charges it. He says his unnecessary call-outs dropped dramatically once he started to charge.

I find just the threat works with most tenants; if you allow them to be arrogant, lazy and stupid without consequences, some will be. That all changes, and very much to your financial advantage, once you introduce a fee. To be fair, the fee must be effectively communicated to the tenant and clearly spelt out beforehand. I put this in my Tenancy Pack, which clearly explains the charges to the tenant, and this is signed by them before they take up occupation; they are given a copy and a copy is also in the room in the tenants' Welcome Pack. Copies of both documents are contained in my *HMO Forms and Documents* manual only available from www.hmodaddy.com.

RETURN:

If applied fairly and clearly, this helps to create a hassle-free time. Priceless!

TOP TIP 26
Shop Using the Web

It is tempting to use your local supplier, but you can save a fortune by just checking web suppliers for what you want, especially if you are spending a lot of money or require regular supplies. Yes, the web is often inconvenient, but once you get into the habit you can begin to appreciate the benefits. If you don't believe me, and want to spoil your day, check out what you could have saved with your last three large purchases!

RETURN:

Massive savings.

TOP TIP 27
Charge Other Landlords a Tenant Finding Fee

If you have more tenants chasing your accommodation than you have accommodation, you could monetise the extra enquiries by selling the leads to other landlords you know who want tenants. Be very careful in your recommendations, as you do not want your reputation tarnished by tenants having a bad experience with the landlord you recommended and the tenants blaming you.

I do the reverse and offer £50, or even more, to others who send me tenants. You need to be absolutely clear as to when you are paid commission; otherwise you are unlikely to get it.

RETURN:

More free money!

TOP TIP 28
Charge Extra for Services and Furniture

You can charge extra for such things as cleaning, bedding, linen, items of furniture, TVs, etc. There is a view that by keeping your rent low, you can attract more tenants. So instead of including such things as cleaning, TV, etc. in your rent, charge them as an extra. You could even charge for furniture. The charges must be clearly specified, and be careful of entering into a contract of hire as you could run foul of the Consumer Credit Act. If the extras are offered as part of the rent, and one figure is put into the contract as rent, you should get around that problem.

I provide a basic level of furnishing, e.g. curtains, carpets, lampshades, bed, bedding, chest of drawers and easy chair, and charge for anything else, but it must be taken as part of the rent. I charge the following for extras:

TV (N.B. reception is not guaranteed)	£3.00 per week
DVD player	£1.00 per week
Washing Machine*	£10.00 per week
Tumble Dryer*	£5.00 per week
Washer/Dryer*	£15.00 per week
Ironing Board & Iron	50p per week
Hoover	£1.00 per week
Baby Bedding	£3.00 per week

Microwave	£1.00 per week
Combi-oven	£2.00 per week
Electric Kettle	FOC
Freezer	£2.00 per week
Fridge	£2.00 per week
Electric Fat Cooker	FOC (£20 deposit)
Wireless Headphones	FOC (£15.00 deposit)
Bedding (Quilt, Cover, Sheet & pillow)	£25.00
Kitchen set (Pots, Cooking utensils Cutlery, Plates & Cups)	£25.00

*Only if there are facilities to fit

The paperwork for the above is available in my *HMO Forms Pack*, only available from www.hmodaddy.com

RETURN:

Depends on what you charge and what the tenants want, but whatever you charge, if you previously provided it in the rent, it is free money!

TOP TIP 29
Charge tenants for storage

With many properties there is available storage space—for example, garages, sheds, cellars, lofts, yards, etc. You can charge tenants or others for their use. Garages are my favourite; I charge £10 pw for the use of a garage. It is essential you have a contract for providing storage, with appropriate safeguards, otherwise you could end up with a garage full of stuff and a problem with what to do with it. I have such an agreement for the use of storage areas in my *Forms Pack* available from www.hmodaddy.com which you are free to use without liability.

RETURN:

Depends on what you have and what you charge—but whatever you charge, it is free money!

TOP TIP 30
Buy End of Range

If you are doing or plan to do renovation work, you will save a small fortune by buying end-of-range, liquidated stock from stores, discount warehouses and auction houses, etc. Invest the time checking out places that specialise in selling such things and also be prepared to negotiate hard. These places expect you to bargain, so do not be afraid to do so.

I buy kitchen units, bathroom fittings, radiators, carpets, etc. Know what you want, what it will cost, and appreciate that you will often have to have transport to collect it. Normally, I will only buy to use in the foreseeable future if I save at least 50% of what I would pay if I were to buy to order.

RETURN:

50% or more on purchasing cost.

TOP TIP 31
Charge a Tenancy Renewal Fee

Unusually, this is one tip I do not do myself, which is to charge a fee for renewing the tenancy. Most HMO landlords grant a six-month Assured Shorthold Tenancy agreement (AST), so when it expires you can charge for renewing it. Fees I have seen vary between £40 to £120.

RETURN:

It depends on how many stay for more than six months—say five do renew and you charge £60 that makes another £300 per year per HMO.

TOP TIP 32
Don't Waste Money on Maintenance Contracts

Maintenance contracts, insurance, breakdown cover, whatever you call it rarely pays for itself. If it were any good why do businesses sell it, as it would not make them money. Gas boiler cover is the main culprit—you could buy a new boiler every three years for what you pay for the insurance. It may be worth paying extra and buying a boiler with a seven or 10-year warranty, rather than paying for an annual maintenance contract.

RETURN:

A new boiler every three to four years.

TOP TIP 33
Increase the Rent for Problem Tenants

If you have a problem tenant, then you can bring home to them their inconvenience by substantially increasing their rent. This may go towards compensating you for the extra work such tenants cause you and send a warning to other tenants. You will probably find that other tenants appreciate you doing this—if they are a problem to you, then they will be a problem for others as well.

Rent increases have to be done properly; otherwise they can be successfully challenged. I deal with how to increase rents in my *DIY Eviction* manual only available from www.hmodaddy.com.

RETURN:

Profit from problem tenants or they leave.

TOP TIP 34
Make Life Easy for Yourself

A bit of a contradiction this one, because it means tearing up this book and putting your feet up. You will probably only be able to do this when you have paid off or substantially paid down your mortgages, and have a good income from your HMOs. What you are looking for is an easy life where the management of your properties takes very little time. To achieve this, you will need content, long-stay tenants who pay automatically—a bit like the tenants in Top Tip 24: Go for DSS—who rarely complain, want very little and stay for life. A trip to your HMO will be like visiting old friends and will rarely require anything else. To be in this situation, you need to not make any changes unless requested by your tenants, and only increase rent when re-letting.

RETURN:

Tranquility. Priceless!

TOP TIP 35
Learn to Self-Evaluate

I have kept what I think is the very best tip until last. By the time you get to this tip, and probably well before, you no doubt have come to the realisation you knew much of what I have said or could have worked it out for yourself—so why haven't you? This is your business and you make out of it what you put in. We have been induced by the education system not to think for ourselves and to follow the pack. In this and in any other business, it is the innovators who do well. Develop a critical review process of what you do, and do things that minimise work and maximise income.

RETURN:

Unlimited wealth and personal satisfaction.

BONUS TIP

I wish I had read my own book before I started my HMO business; I would have made and saved a fortune. Unfortunately, I have had to learn through trial and error—these tips have been learnt from over 20 years' experience. I hope you feel you have benefitted enormously from reading this.

If you do not agree that you have not received at least 100 times the cost of this book in savings or value, please ask for your money back!

Please feel free to share any other money-making or saving tips you have with me, and thank you for reading my book.

All the very best for the future.

HMO DADDY RUNS COURSES:

- Options to HMOs
- Tour of HMOs
- How to Convert a Property Into an HMO
- DIY Eviction
- Mega HMO Course

For further details please visit my website www.hmodaddy.com or call 0121 526 6410.

THE AUTHOR

HMO Daddy, Jim Haliburton, is a star of the BBC show 'Meet The Landlords', author of over 10 books and manuals including *How to Become a Multi-Millionaire HMO Landlord* and regularly writes articles for property magazines.

He began investing in property in 1991, letting rooms to students, while he was a college law lecturer.

By 2004, he decided to leave his job and buy investment properties full-time. He now owns a letting office as well as over 100 HMOs, 30 single-lets and has 24 Rent-to-Rents.

He is also in regular demand as a speaker at property meetings around the UK, and runs courses and mentorships on the business of being a HMO landlord. He is unique in the business in that he lets people work in his property business to learn the skills of being an HMO landlord and gives tours of his properties.

I WANT TO HEAR FROM YOU

As a reader of the first edition of my book on *Thirty-Five Money Making or Saving Tips for HMO Landlords* you are the most important critic and commentator. I value your opinion and comments. I want to know what else you would like me to include in the book, what you disagree with and any other words of wisdom you wish me to share.

I would like feedback from you, my readers, both positive and negative. Any improvements I can incorporate to help other landlords through the maze of being an HMO landlord will be gratefully received, and I am sure will receive the gratitude of landlords I pass them onto.

I welcome your comments and you can email or write to me to let me know what you did or did not like about my book, as well as what I can do to make it better, or what other information or services I can provide.

I also provide training courses on all aspects of the business, which you can find out about on my website www.hmodaddy.com.

When you write to me please include your name, email, address and phone number. I assure you, I will value and review your comments.

Jim Haliburton, author

Email: jim@hmodaddy.com

Website: www.hmodaddy.com

Mail: Jim Haliburton
        14 Walsall Road
        Wednesbury
        West Midlands
        WS10 9JL

Printed in Great Britain
by Amazon.co.uk, Ltd.,
Marston Gate.